This book is dedicated to:
My parents, Rav and Karen
My brother, Yehuda
My wife, Monica
Our children, David, Joshua,
and Miriam

THE

SECRET

UNLOCKING THE SOURCE OF JOY & FULFILLMENT

THE
SECRET

UNLOCKING THE SOURCE OF JOY & FULFILLMENT

MICHAEL BERG

www.kabbalah.com™

For further information:
The Kabbalah Centre

155 E. 48th St., New York City, NY 10017
1062 S. Robertson Blvd., Los Angeles, CA 90035

1-800-Kabbalah
www.kabbalah.com

First Edition October 2002
Second Edition May 2004. Printed in USA

ISBN 1-57189-314-8

TABLE OF CONTENTS

ACKNOWLEDGMENTS

I would like to thank all those who have made this book possible.

First and foremost, I am grateful to Rav Yehuda Ashlag, who first began revealing The Secret;

My parents, Rav and Karen Berg, who enabled me to discover and explore The Secret, and who continue to teach The Secret to me by living it every day;

My brother, Yehuda—together, may we merit to reveal The Secret to the world;

My wife, Monica—our love has grown so much, and may it continue to grow stronger and stronger forever;

Our Children, David, Joshua, and Miriam—you are my constant inspiration to reveal The Secret, so that you will grow up in a world where joy and fulfillment are achieved by all humanity;

Mitch Sisskind, Peter Guzzardi, and Esther Sibilia, who worked so long on this short book.

PROLOGUE

As *The Secret* was going into final production, my
wife and I were blessed with the arrival of our second son, Joshua. We were overjoyed when he joined
us in this physical world on April 6, 2002. A few
hours after he was born, the doctors informed my
wife and me of their concern that Joshua might have
Down syndrome. As any parents would be, we were
shocked.

In the time since then, we have met many wonderful people in the Down syndrome parent commu-
nity. Some of these are people we chose to meet,
and others we might never have encountered if cir-
cumstances had been different. I would like to
thank all of these helpful and beautiful souls.

We have learned so much from this opportunity.
Perhaps some day we will write a book on the lessons
it has taught us. For any parent of a special needs
child, I would like to recommend *Expecting Adam*,

by Martha Beck. It will inspire you, and I believe it will bring you joy and peace.

In keeping with the brevity that was one of our goals for this book, I want to share these few words on how greatly this experience has strengthened my understanding of The Secret and its power. For us, The Secret has transformed what might have been a troubling time into something that is beautiful, joyful, and, I strongly believe, forever fulfilling.

I had always believed that The Secret can transform every area of one's life, but now I know it. Without a doubt, no matter what situation you find yourself in, learning and living The Secret can and will bring your life the endless joy and fulfillment that you deserve and are meant to have.

Blessings and Light,

Michael Berg
June 20, 2002

CHAPTER ONE

BEGINNINGS

The true origins of this book lie in the distant past, in the ancient wisdom known as Kabbalah. I was raised in the teachings of Kabbalah, and I learned to see them as the heritage and birthright of humanity. The book's more immediate beginnings, however, trace back to a series of conversations between two men in the city of Jerusalem more than eighty years ago. One of the men was a spiritual master, the other his student.

The younger man who had recently arrived in Jerusalem from Eastern Europe was named Yehuda Ashlag. In the years that followed he would be known as Rav Ashlag, recognized as one of Kabbalah's greatest scholars. Just as importantly, he would be loved and appreciated for his joy and goodness, which touched everyone whom he met.

The name of the older man has never been revealed, and mystery still surrounds that first meeting. In a letter many years later, Rav Ashlag wrote only that a stranger had come to his home one day and asked to speak with him. Nothing in the stranger's appearance suggested that he was a spiritual person. His dress and his manner were typical of the merchant class. But from their first conversations, Rav Ashlag knew that his guest possessed the wisdom of the Creator.

Master and student began studying together. Almost every night, over a period of several months, they met at the master's home. As Rav Ashlag recalled, most of these sessions focused on the struggle between creative and destructive forces in the world and on the role of the Creator in this seemingly endless conflict. Rav Ashlag raised questions that people have been asking for centuries:

- Why are we in the world?

- What is the purpose of our lives?

- How can we find fulfillment in a world afflicted with pain and suffering?

Whenever the student posed these questions, his inquiries were gently deflected by the master. Finally, Rav Ashlag began to plead openly for answers, and at last his teacher did reveal the ancient wisdom that lies at the heart of this book. In later writings, Rav Ashlag would express his overwhelming joy at receiving the profound insights his master had shared with him.

But not long after this revelation, Rav Ashlag noticed a change in his teacher. His voice became weak and his manner tentative.

One night, when the older man seemed especially frail, Rav Ashlag remained at his bedside—and at dawn his master passed from this world. As Rav Ashlag wrote:

I cannot express the immensity of my sadness. Even what I had learned from him was almost forgotten, due to the greatness of my grief. It was only the compassion of the Creator that allowed me to recall the great teachings that I had received from this great master—who, to those around him, was known only as a successful and trustworthy businessman. Not a single person to this day has been made aware of the wisdom that he disclosed to me. Nor did he give me permission to reveal his name.

From the day I first read of these meetings between Rav Ashlag and his spiritual master, there was one question I absolutely had to answer: What was the lesson—the wisdom—that Rav Ashlag received? In the pages that follow I will share with you the answer that I found in Rav Ashlag's own writings, as well as in the ancient legends and teachings of Kabbalah. I call this wisdom The Secret, and when you truly understand The Secret and take it to heart, your life will forever be transformed.

The Secret, however, did not appear in one stunning moment of revelation. It did not exist as a sentence or a paragraph in Rav Ashlag's writings, nor to the best of my knowledge was it something he ever said. Somehow The Secret was present both everywhere and nowhere. It became clear to me only after years of study. And in the course of solving this puzzle, I discovered many more great teachings of Kabbalah—lessons that not only brought me closer to

The Secret, but allowed me to understand and use it once I found it.

One of these lessons needs to be introduced now, for it's the foundation of everything that follows. This lesson can be expressed in few words: Our true destiny is not the pain and suffering that can seem so pervasive in the world but a joy and fulfillment beyond imagining.

As with many Kabbalistic teachings over the centuries, this lesson, which many people live their lives without ever understanding, has been best expressed in stories and tales such as the one that follows.

THE UNEXPECTED GUEST

Hundreds of years ago, somewhere in Eastern Europe, there lived a very poor man and his wife. Their names were Josef and Rebecca, and their home was little more than a shack. Their only possession was a single, scrawny cow, from whose milk and cheese they fed themselves and earned a meager living.

One afternoon, not long before sundown, Josef heard a knock on the door, and when he opened it, his jaw dropped in astonishment. Standing before him was the man known far and wide as the greatest Kabbalist in the world, the man known as the Baal Shem Tov—"the master of the holy name." He was accompanied by a few of his students, who stood respectfully behind him.

"We've been traveling all day, and now it is almost sundown," said the Baal Shem Tov. "May we join you for the evening meal?"

"Of course, of course," said Josef, standing aside as the master and his students entered the shack. At that moment, Rebecca, who was standing at the stove, looked over her shoulder. She too was astonished, and even a bit frightened, by the sudden appearance of the great master.

"Very well then," said the Baal Shem Tov, glancing around. "But I have to tell you that my students and I are very hungry after our travels. We'd like some fine cuts of meat, some fresh vegetables, and of course some good wine. You can accommodate us, can't you?"

Josef hesitated, but then nodded enthusiastically. "Oh yes, oh yes," he said. "This is a great honor for us, and we want to give you exactly what you desire. Let me just speak with my wife for a moment...."

He and Rebecca retired to a

corner of the room. "What are we going to do?" Rebecca asked anxiously. "How are we going to give these men what they want? We have no meat or fresh vegetables, and the wine we drink isn't at all worthy of the Baal Shem Tov!"

Josef thought for a moment. Then he said, "There's only one thing to do. I'll have to sell the cow in order to buy food. There's no time to waste!" And before his wife could protest, he hurried out the door.

Within the hour, Josef returned with supplies for exactly the sort of meal the Baal Shem Tov had described, and Rebecca hurried to prepare it. But as the great Kabbalist began to eat, Josef and Rebecca were amazed at how he ate and ate, and drank and drank. As soon as he finished one plate, he immediately called for more. He was like an eating machine! Even the students were amazed. It was as if the Baal Shem Tov intended to eat the poor to the poor couple out of house and home—and that was exactly what was happening!

After downing the last morsel, the Baal Shem Tov pushed his chair back from the table and got to his feet. "That was delicious! Thank you very much," he said. "Now we have renewed energy for the road, so we will be on our way." And in a flash, he and his students were gone just as suddenly as they had arrived.

"Well, this is a fine mess," said Rebecca, when the door had closed behind the departing visitors. "Now we really have nothing, not even that scrawny cow! What are we going to do, Josef? We're going to starve!"

Unable to bear the sight of his weeping wife, and having no idea what to do, Josef opened the door and stepped out into the cold night air. Soon he found himself walking through the forest, with no real idea of where he was going. How was he going to solve the terrible dilemma he and Rebecca were now facing? Then, without thinking, he closed his eyes, fell to his knees, and began to pray. From the bottom of his heart he prayed for all the things he had never had—not just for himself, but for his long-suffering wife as well.

Just then, Josef heard a rustling in the branches behind him, and as he opened his eyes he saw someone stagger into the clearing. It was an old man, well dressed but disheveled, who had obviously been drinking. But as he caught sight of Josef, his eyes shone with happiness.

"I'm so glad there's someone here," said the old man, slurring his words. "I don't want to die alone."

"Die?" said Josef, getting to his feet. "You're not going to die. You've just had a bit too much to drink."

But as Josef reached out to steady the newcomer, the old man sighed and sank to the ground. As Josef knelt beside him, the man told a painfully sad story. He was very wealthy, but his money was the only thing his family cared about. In fact, they were, like vultures, just waiting for him to die so they could get their hands on his fortune.

"But they're in for a surprise," said the old man, with a rueful smile. "They don't know that I've buried the treasure right here in this forest. They'll get nothing because they deserve nothing!"

"I'm sorry this has happened to you," Josef replied. "It's cold out here, and you need a warm place to rest."

The old man just shook his head. "It's too late for that," he said. "But you've been so kind to me. That's something that hasn't happened in many years, so I will repay your kindness. Here.... Look..."

But as he reached into the pocket of his coat, he began coughing. Then, just as suddenly, he fell silent and his eyes closed. Josef quickly bent to help him, but sure enough, the man was dead.

Now Josef felt more frightened and confused than ever. Yet as he stared at the body beside him, he saw that in the instant before he died the old man had withdrawn a slip of paper from his pocket. Josef gently took hold of the paper and unfolded it. To his amazement, it was a map—and when he followed it, he discovered a buried treasure beyond anything he could have imagined!

Five years passed. One day the Baal Shem Tov and his students were again on the road when a fine carriage passed headed in the other direction. As the students looked into the carriage, they were amazed to see the poor man who had struggled to provide them with dinner years before. Sitting beside him was his wife, and they both looked not only as if they were wealthy, but as if they didn't have a care in the world!

When the students turned to their master for some explanation, the Baal Shem Tov only smiled calmly, as if this is what he had expected all along. "You see," he said to the students, "it was Josef's destiny to be joyful and fulfilled, but he never thought to ask for everything that was really meant for him. He would have been content to spend the rest of his life with his one scrawny cow. That's why I had to help him get rid of it."

In this tale, the scrawny cow is a metaphor for the life we are willing to accept, while the abundance is the gift that becomes ours when we live The Secret. Although the tale describes this abundance in material terms, the scrawny cow and the fine carriage are really symbols of spiritual levels of being.

Kabbalah teaches that *nothing* of a material nature can bring us lasting joy—not because there's anything inherently wrong with material objects and desires, but because our true needs are so much greater. The pleasures of sex, food, and luxury offer only a tantalizing hint of what awaits us at the source of true joy, which explains why we are always searching for more. We imagine a quantitative solution to the search—that we need only to get more of what we already have—but the fulfillment that the Creator intends for us is *qualitatively* different from anything the physical realm can offer.

In my own life, becoming a parent has given me some insight into what this qualitative difference really means. As I write, my son David is almost three years old. My wife, Monica, gave birth to David in a Los Angeles hospital at around four o'clock in the morning. As overwhelmed and exhausted as I was that day, something came over me that I'm sure every new parent can identify with: a feeling of *inexpressible* joy. I knew I would love my son, and I also sensed that it might be a different kind of love than I had known in the past. But as I tried to envision what this parental love would be like, I had no choice but to see it in terms of what I had already experienced. I thought it would be the same, but more so. Later I realized that the change was *qualitative* rather than just *quantitative*. It was a new kind of love—not just bigger, but different. I realized this joy is what the Creator intends for all of us all the time. I had been given just a tiny glimpse of it, enough so that I wanted to make that joy a constant in my life, and in my wife's, and in my child's—and I wanted to bring it to the whole world as well.

The truth is, the potential for this joy exists within each of us. Discovering it lies within our grasp, but somehow we have lost our way. I am convinced that there is one reason we have not yet fulfilled the Creator's desire for us: *because we don't know The Secret*. As a result, we literally see the world backward, as if we were trying to start a car by letting the air out of the tires or trying to boil an egg by putting it in the refrigerator. No wonder so many of us become discouraged about finding joy in life—or even give up entirely.

You may be surprised at how easily The Secret can be expressed, how few words this great teaching requires. But as you continue, you'll come to see how The Secret requires a fundamental transformation in how we think, feel, and live. At the same time, you'll begin to understand the absolute joy and fulfillment that The Secret will bring into your life. Conveying what "absolute joy and fulfillment" means is one of this book's biggest challenges—and I want to be very clear that the joy Kabbalah describes does not mean euphoria or anything like it. It's something much richer, something that comes from deep within rather than outside. It's the realization of your true inner nature. It's what you've always been looking for. Fulfillment, then, lies not so much in finding the gift as it does in realizing that you've had it all along. Please keep this in mind as you turn the page to read The Secret.

THE SECRET

**THE ONLY WAY TO ACHIEVE
TRUE JOY AND FULFILLMENT
IS BY BECOMING
A BEING OF SHARING.**

Now that you've read The Secret, you may wonder, Can the essence of life really be this simple? In fact, you may be thinking that you already perform many acts of sharing and other "good deeds." In that light, you may wonder why a joyous and fulfilled life continues to elude you. If so, take a moment to really think about this. Please consider the possibility that, like Josef, you may have underestimated the joy that the Creator intends for you. In the same way, you may find that The Secret's definition of sharing differs from your everyday understanding of the word. Notice, also, that The Secret does not mention specific acts of sharing or instances of kindness. The Secret speaks of a process of change, an experience of becoming, a fundamental transformation from one kind of being to another.

In everyday life we are taught in countless ways that getting is the path to fulfillment, but The Secret tells us something different. Regarding this point, I discovered an amazing tale in the writings of Rav Ashlag.

CANDLES AND DIAMONDS

Long ago, there was a poor candlemaker named Jacob. He heard of a mysterious island where diamonds were as common as ordinary pebbles. So Jacob left his home and set out for the nearest seaport. There he learned that the island of diamonds really did exist, but he would have to hurry. A boat sailed to the island only once every seven years, and it was leaving immediately! So Jacob rushed aboard.

When he arrived on the island, he found that what he'd heard was all true! Diamonds were everywhere, like sand on the seashore. Falling to his knees, Jacob began filling his bags with the glittering gems, dreaming of how rich he was going to be back home.

Just then, however, one of the inhabitants of the island approached him. "You're wasting your time filling your bags with those worthless pebbles," said the newcomer. "Since you're going to be here for seven years, you'd better have a way to support yourself. Do you have a trade?"

"Why, I'm a candlemaker," said Jacob.

"Very well. Then you'd better start making candles."

That is exactly what Jacob did, and very soon he had a thriving business. In fact, since there were no other candlemakers to compete with, he became the most important man on the island. Almost before Jacob knew it, seven years had passed—and one day the boat arrived.

So Jacob hurriedly packed up all his possessions and jumped onboard. When he returned home his family eagerly looked in his suitcases and then stared at Jacob in amazement. "Where is all the treasure?" asked his wife and children. "You were gone for seven years, and all you've brought back is a bunch of candles!"

Jacob just laughed. Didn't they understand? Candles had made him an important man on the island! But as he opened his mouth to speak, the truth suddenly dawned on him. He had forgotten the purpose for which he'd gone to the island—and now he had nothing more valuable than when he left.

In discussing this tale, Rav Ashlag explains that this physical world is an island we are visiting. The diamonds are the opportunities for giving and sharing that exist all around us. Because they are as numerous as grains of sand on a beach, we become oblivious to them under the seemingly urgent needs that life in the everyday world imposes on us. Caught up in the values of the "island," we easily forget the real purpose for which we have come here. We are here to live in joy and fulfillment.

Achieving that destiny requires profound transformation. We must change the foundation of our being from getting to giving—not only in what we do, but in who we are. This is the key to making The Secret the foundation of our lives.

Not long ago there was a moderate earthquake in Los Angeles. In the middle of the night, I was awakened by the creaking and swaying of our house. Without thinking, my wife and I instantly ran into our son's room to lift him out of his crib. I'm sure parents all over the city were doing the same thing at that moment. On the purely physical level, I suppose what propelled us out of our beds was the neural impulse that activated the muscles of our legs. But from a Kabbalistic perspective, the essence of sharing had moved us—for sharing is first and foremost an *inner* condition.

More specifically, sharing as described by The Secret looks beyond external reference points. Sharing matters not because it allows us to perform conspicuously good deeds or to be recognized as righteous people. Sharing matters because by transforming ourselves into *sharing beings*, we gain the joy and fulfillment that is life's true purpose. The purpose of this book is to reveal what it means to live as a sharing person and to explore the profound change it requires.

The more I studied the works of Rav Ashlag, the more I understood what becoming a being of sharing means—and I recognized the transformation in Rav Ashlag himself, as it emerged from his writings. At the same time, I was blessed that my parents, Rav Berg and Karen Berg, provided real-life examples of transformative sharing, both in the depth of their understanding and in the way they lived and continue to live every day. By dedicating their lives to bringing the teachings of Kabbalah to the world, they took a key step in a process that has spanned many centuries: that is, the gradual unveiling of Kabbalistic teachings and the transformation of Kabbalah from a body of hidden wisdom to a set of powerful and practical tools for realizing true joy. They worked every day to make this happen, and their work continues. Even with all the challenges it entailed, growing up in this environment was a great gift.

And now I see an opportunity—even a responsibility—to take another step forward. When I understood with clarity The Secret and its message of sharing, which embodies all the wisdom of Kabbalah in a single concept, I knew that I must spread it as widely and as quickly as I possibly could.

Now you know why—and from where—this book has come into being. In the pages that follow, we'll look at what The Secret really means, not only as an idea or a teaching, but as a tool for improving your life infinitely.

BEGINNINGS

CHAPTER TWO

ONENESS

In order to really *live* our lives in The Secret, rather than just *spend* them in the misguided pursuit of one distraction after another, we need to understand the logical sequence of thought from which The Secret develops. While The Secret expresses itself in just one sentence, those few words provide the summation of a three-part logical progression at the heart of Kabbalistic wisdom.

1. The only way for us to achieve fulfillment is by achieving oneness with the Creator, the source of all joy and fulfillment.

2. Oneness with the Creator is achieved by becoming like Him *in our essence*—for spiritual oneness is accomplished through similarity of spiritual form.

3. The Creator's essence is one of sharing. Therefore, to become like Him, we need to transform our essence and nature from one of *receiving* to one of sharing.

Let's look at these ideas one by one.

I

THE ONLY WAY FOR US TO ACHIEVE FULFILLMENT IS BY ACHIEVING ONENESS WITH THE CREATOR, THE SOURCE OF ALL JOY AND FULFILLMENT.

In order to gain the joy and fulfillment that we want, we need to know both its true source and how we can connect to that source. Kabbalah teaches that every instance of happiness, whether the small satisfaction of a task well done at work or the great joy that accompanies the birth of a child, has its source in the Creator. The only way to connect to that source in the Creator, the Kabbalists explain, is by achieving oneness with the Creator.

In Rav Ashlag's own words:

> *This oneness is expressed by our sages through the simple word "cleaving" (as in "cleaving to"). This word is not often used, and to a large extent its meaning has been lost. It implies both the loftiness of the Creator and the worthiness of that lowly creature, man, to draw close to Him. Consider this word carefully, and you will be able to evaluate the relationship whereby one cleaves to the other. Then you will understand why the sages use this word as representing the purpose of this creation.*

At first glance, this passage may seem somewhat abstract, but we have all experienced what Rav Ashlag means. We all know people whom we like to be around. Their energy rubs off on us. When we're with them, we feel not only happy but somehow changed, so that the stressful details of life no longer seem to affect us. Closeness with the Creator offers something similar to, but exponentially greater than, this kind of human relationship. It offers *oneness* with the source of all goodness, abundance, protection, and unconditional love. Try to remember a moment from your own life when all that is good and right with the world seemed to express itself through you and another person—when the forces of the universe converged, and for one second all was perfect and complete and secure. That is just a glimpse, the great Kabbalists say, of the feeling of oneness with the Creator.

This simple but very beautiful story conveys the feeling.

THE BAKER AND THE BEGGAR

Long ago, there lived a baker who one day happened to bake an unusually beautiful loaf of bread—so beautiful and so perfect that it seemed to come from the hand of the Creator Himself. Rather than sell it, the baker decided to take the bread to the synagogue as an offering to the Creator who had made such a perfect loaf of bread possible.

Alone in the sanctuary, the baker opened the sacred ark and gently placed the loaf of bread inside. He prayed for the Creator to accept his offering, and then he departed.

Just at that moment, a beggar happened to be passing by the synagogue. It had been a long time since he'd had anything to eat, and he felt as if he might die of starvation at any moment. Yet somehow he could not believe that this fate was what the Creator had intended for him. So he entered the synagogue and quietly made his way to the sanctuary. Kneeling before the ark, he explained his plight to the Creator.

As soon as he'd completed his prayer, the beggar opened the ark, and there was the beautiful loaf of bread! Murmuring a new prayer of thanks, the beggar lifted the bread and hurried from the synagogue.

For his part, the baker was wondering whether his offering to the Creator had been accepted, and he couldn't resist returning to find out. When he opened the ark and saw that the bread was gone, his heart leaped with joy. In fact, he resolved to make a new offering every week of a perfectly baked loaf of bread.

As it happened, whenever the baker placed a new offering in the ark, the beggar once again found himself in desperate need of food. Time and again, the beggar prayed before the ark, and then opened it to find a new loaf of bread. Time and again, the baker returned to see if his offering had been accepted and was overjoyed to discover that the ark was empty. Both men, for different reasons, felt that their prayers had been answered and that they were at one with the Creator. This exchange

went on for fourteen years, and
not once did the beggar arrive
before the baker to find the ark
empty.

This is the beauty and sim-
plicity with which the Creator fulfills our desires.

Today we might dismiss this tale as a
series of mere coincidences. It can hardly
represent the exalted spiritual connection
that the baker and the beggar ascribe to it,
because it concerns only two humble people
exchanging a commodity that can be bought
on almost any street corner. Surely an
authentic spiritual experience must take
place on the scale of Noah's flood or the
parting of the Red Sea. But in commentaries
on this story, Kabbalists tell us that the tale
indeed offers a great example of oneness
with the Creator, by describing an experience we can have at any moment, or at every

moment, in a very simple way. Authentic spiritual connection depends on desiring the connection, *intending* it, and embracing it when it takes place.

2

ONENESS WITH THE CREATOR IS ACHIEVED BY BECOMING LIKE HIM *IN OUR ESSENCE*—FOR SPIRITUAL ONENESS IS ACCOMPLISHED THROUGH SIMILARITY OF SPIRITUAL FORM.

Kabbalah teaches that spiritual closeness cannot be measured in units of time or distance. Spiritual closeness means similarity of form. So we gain closeness—ultimately oneness—with the Creator by making our essence identical to His.

Kabbalah teaches us that sharing is the essence of the Creator. We become one with the Creator when sharing becomes our essence as well. Likeness of spiritual form with the Creator depends not on how well you know the Bible, where you worship, how much you suffer, how often you pray, what you eat, or how much of your income you give away. Oneness with the Creator depends on what's in your soul, and how your soul expresses itself in the world. Oneness with the Creator exists not just when you share, but when you become a *being of sharing*.

As Rav Ashlag put it:

> *Our sages have asked what it means to "cleave unto Him." How is it possible to cleave unto the Creator, for He is a consuming fire? They answered that one should cleave to His attributes. Just as He is merciful, we too should be merciful. Just as He is giving, we too should be giving. The degree to which two things are similar is the measure of cleaving,*

and the degree of dissimilarity is the measure of separation. Consider, for example, two people who hate one another. We say that they are "far apart." And if they love one another, we say they are "of one flesh." Here we are not speaking of spatial proximity or distance. Instead, we refer to an inner similarity of form. As a result of our emulating the Creator's attributes, we cleave to Him. All of the Creator's actions are to impart to and help others and are not for His own sake. In the same way, all our actions must be to impart to and help others. In this manner, we will be similar to Him and attain oneness with Him.

Several times, I've found myself in situations that explain exactly what is meant by "oneness with Him." A conversation had been going on among a group of people, and I found that I simply couldn't take part in it. I wasn't angry or bored, but I felt I had nothing in common with the others that would have allowed me to connect with them. You've probably had this experience yourself. On the other hand, when you do share something with people—the way you think, or how you feel, or what you do—you experience a closeness that not only helps you communicate, but makes you feel a part of one another's lives. With regard to the Creator, this closeness is what Rav Ashlag means by the word *cleaving*. But it's not something that we can passively wait for or expect. We need to initiate this closeness by making the attributes of the Creator our attributes as well. We need to emulate the Creator's essence in the thoughts and actions of our daily lives.

3

THE CREATOR'S ESSENCE IS ONE OF SHARING. THEREFORE, TO BECOME LIKE HIM, WE NEED TO TRANSFORM OUR ESSENCE AND NATURE FROM ONE OF *RECEIVING* TO ONE OF SHARING.

Rav Ashlag explains:

> *We can now look at the purpose of creation, that is, "cleaving" to His true countenance. This is nothing more than the leaves imitating their root. Joy is nothing more than the creation imitating its Creator. When they are equal in every respect, then we have joy. On the other hand, anything that happens to us from*

things disconnected from our root becomes painful, a burden to the soul, and even unbearable. We can conclude that our entire hope of fulfillment depends on the degree to which we cause the nature of our leaves to imitate that of our root.

Our root is the Creator, whose essence is sharing—but our daily lives can distance us from our own true nature. Getting instead of giving can become an ingrained reflex. So it's time to challenge and question that reflex. We need to move in a counterintuitive way from what we've been *taught* by the material world to what *we know* in the foundation of our souls. We need to reeducate ourselves from the idea that joy comes from receiving to the understanding that real joy comes only from sharing, which is the essence of our very souls.

Every act of giving and sharing brings us closer to the Creator. The more you share, the more your essence and His become one. But there's more to this concept: As your understanding deepens, you see that joy and fulfillment increase in proportion to the difficulty of sharing.

At the start of our work with The Secret, virtually anything we do of a sharing nature has a positive, exhilarating effect. But as with physical exercise, continued growth requires greater effort. We need to make sharing more challenging—and the world being what it is, there is certainly no shortage of challenges.

Transformative sharing changes not only what you do but who you are. If such transformation seems like a lot to ask, let me assure you that you have everything you need to make it happen. After all, transforming who you are doesn't mean becoming something outside your nature. It means rediscovering your true nature, who you *really* are. The spark of the Creator is already within you. You just need to fan that flame through positive actions of sharing.

Sharing will become easier if you're always aware of the real goal toward which all positive change is directed. Not "righteousness" or "enlightenment" or any other self-help or New Age buzzword, the purpose of sharing is to become a being of sharing. Why? Simply because our own joy and fulfillment expands as this transformation takes place. In this way, it's self-interest in the highest sense.

ONENESS

CHAPTER THREE

TRANSFORMATIVE SHARING

The level of change in your life that The Secret implies is truly fundamental. Yet to begin, you don't need to change anything except the consciousness with which you perform the actions of your daily life.

Imagine that you're a parent making dinner for your family. What is the mental framework in which you see that activity? You may understand it as a routine obligation, another chore. But you can also make a choice to see yourself performing an act of sharing for your family. When you do so, nothing changes in terms of what you're doing, but everything changes in how you frame your action.

You're no longer thinking, "I'll do this chore because it's the right thing to do, and somebody's got to do it." Instead, you endow your action with a genuine sharing intention, and you see it as assisting you toward becoming a sharing human being. This small change in your way of thinking can be the first step toward transformation of your whole life.

Once this process of reframing has become established, you're ready for sharing actions that take you out of your comfort zone. The more challenging sharing is, the more transforming it will be.

Suppose a successful executive announces a $5 million donation to build a library at the state university. No doubt that's a wonderful thing for the students, but what's really crucial for the giver is the transformative energy the gift holds for him or her. What is the significance of $5 million to a person who has $500 million? What is the meaning of a huge gift if rooted in a desire to see one's name carved above the entrance to a building?

If sharing something of which he or she has a great deal, such as money, is easy for the executive, transformative sharing might involve something of which he or she has less, such as personal time. It may even mean creating an entirely new category of experience—something that he or she has never done or even thought of doing. Kabbalah teaches that we are not in the world just to do the things that come naturally. We are here to expand our nature and thereby strengthen our connection to far richer experience.

Life's challenges are not simply mistakes that the Creator forgot to correct or remove. The obstacles we face have been put in place as part of a thoroughly positive intention, as opportunities for transformative sharing. Yet long before we do anything or give anything, whether money or love or wise counsel, our action is defined by the character of the desire that underlies it—and Kabbalah teaches that true sharing is defined by our desire for spiritual transformation.

Imagine a man who has lived his entire life in a comfortably furnished home with plenty of food and water, but with no access to the outside world. The doors of his house have always been nailed shut, and the windows painted over. He has never seen day or night. All his activities have taken place in a controlled environment.

Because this is the only life he has ever known, he doesn't feel deprived or imprisoned. In fact, he's quite content. But then one day something happens.

The man stares at the front door and notices it's nailed shut. Opening it would be a lot of work, and who knows whether it would be worthwhile? Furthermore, he's always been satisfied with his indoor life. Finally, overcome by curiosity, he decides to pry open the door to see what's on the other side—and it turns out to be more wonderful than anything he could possibly have imagined. The sunlight! The trees swaying in the breeze! It's overwhelming.

From that moment on, his indoor life seems completely unfulfilling. He sees that it was based on a severely limited notion of reality, and he becomes determined to connect again with the limitless magnificence he discovered outside. The difficulty of the task vanishes before the desire for the objective. And whenever he gets another glimmer of light, he desires more.

Like the man who stays inside his house, each of us can be lulled into remaining within our comfort zone. But once we get even a glimpse of real fulfillment, we can no longer feel content with the limited, available pleasures. We've started inexorably down the path to an entirely new, transcendent experience. The difficulties we encounter along this path—the work of pry-ing open the doors and breaking down the walls—become inseparable from the goal. As that work becomes an integral part of moving toward our boldest dreams, obstacles become an enticing part of the journey.

Seen in this light, seemingly important acts of sharing may be insignificant as expressions of The Secret. And the converse is also true: Things that seem minor can prove quite the opposite.

Years ago, when we were both small boys, I remember riding in the back seat of a car with my brother, Yehuda. Both of us were hungry and thirsty, but between us we had only a single stick of chewing gum. At that moment, nothing could have seemed more difficult than giving the stick of gum to my brother, yet even now, many years later, I vividly remember how wonderful and genuinely transforming it felt when I did just that. It was more than the warm feeling of having done a good deed. I felt a real sense of freedom—of leaving behind the restrictions of my human nature.

For me, that was an important stick of gum! The memory has provided me with an invaluable touchstone of what real sharing involves. Transformative sharing is not defined by money or time, but by going against our habits and instincts in order to achieve our true purpose.

Imagine finding a wallet stuffed with hundred-dollar bills. You call its owner and arrange to meet and return it. Afterward you feel strangely unsettled. Why? After all, you've just performed a genuine act of sharing. Then it dawns on you: You're disappointed because you were hoping to be offered a reward. But the truth is, something extremely valuable has been given to you. You've been granted an opportunity to take another step toward the boundless joy and fulfillment that comes from transformative sharing.

Armed with this insight, you might see what you really needed to share—that is, give away—in this situation. It wasn't the wallet. It was the concealed expectation of compensation, or approval, or perhaps even admiration. It was all the forms of ego-based desire that need to be shed in order for true freedom and fulfillment to be gained.

Or imagine a parent whose small child is begging for a piece of candy. Better yet, imagine that the child is begging for a second piece, or a third. If the parent gives in, is this an act of sharing? Strictly speaking, perhaps so. After all, one person has given something to another. But is it an act of transformative sharing? Not really, since it's just the path of least resistance, trading long-term good for a short-term payoff. And that payoff lies not just in quieting the whining child. Perhaps it also includes the self-satisfaction of seeing oneself as a generous parent. In many areas of life lurk hidden agendas that can undermine the true experience of giving. The key is to become aware of all the forces at work in a situation or relationship. Doing so is a matter of committing yourself to following the transformative path.

Whenever the chance for an act of sharing presents itself, ask yourself what you really want. How can you express your desire in a way that is genuinely transformative? And how can you resist the hidden desire for praise or recognition that so often undermines even the most positive actions? The following tale tells of one man's answers to these questions.

YOSELE, THE HOLY MISER

Long ago, on the outskirts of a small town, a wealthy man named Yosele lived by himself in a huge mansion. Although he had more money than he could possibly spend, Yosele was known as a terrible miser. Whenever a poor person appeared at his doorstep begging for a few coins or for something to eat, that person was angrily turned away. It didn't matter how heartbreaking someone's story might be, or how dire his or her need. Yosele never gave anything to anybody.

When Yosele finally died, no tears were shed. He had no family or friends, and nobody was going to miss him. In fact, just knowing that he was up there in his mansion had been oppressive to everyone, and when he was gone the whole town breathed a sigh of relief.

But then something very strange and unexpected happened. One after another, every needy family in town showed up at the home of the town's rabbi, all telling the same story. For many years, on Wednesday evenings, someone had secretly placed envelopes of money under their doors. The families had come to depend on this help every week, but it had suddenly stopped. The people were frightened and confused.

The rabbi, of course, did everything he could to help. But as he listened to one family after another, an astonishing possibility began to dawn on him. Only one thing had happened that could account for the sudden end to the charity that had helped so many people, and that was the death of Yosele. Could the man who portrayed himself as a miser really have been something very different? When night fell, the rabbi retired to his study and prayed for an answer.

So fervent was the rabbi's prayer that his consciousness transcended time and space. He crossed even the boundary of death itself, and he saw the Garden of Eden to which the souls of the righteous return when they have left this world. And there, waiting for him in the Garden, he saw none other than Yosele himself, surrounded by the souls of the patriarchs and matriarchs and the great sages of history.

"Why, Yosele?" the rabbi implored. "Why would you choose to hide the goodness that was in your heart? Why would you adopt the identity of a selfish and mean-spirited person?"

Yosele hesitated, then spoke softly: "I once really was the kind of person you describe. The more I had, the more I wanted. Yet it seemed as if I had everything. And here was the strangest part. The more I got, the more I felt that I was losing. So every day was like climbing a hill made of sand. I was running as fast as I could, but in my own heart I seemed always to be slipping backward. Despite all that I had, I felt like I had nothing. So I certainly had no interest in sharing with anyone else."

At that moment, as he saw Yosele in the sacred Garden, the rabbi suddenly felt that he was beginning to understand. Here was a man whom everyone had called a miser—and he had chosen to perpetuate that image in order to gain his reward in the life to come. The rabbi's heart pounded at the realization of this. "Surely you are blessed beyond measure," he cried. "To be received by these

great souls must indeed be paradise."

A slight smile crossed Yosele's
face. "Yes," he said, looking deep
into the rabbi's eyes, "it is wonderful to be in the presence of the
elect, but there is nothing, nothing, that can compare with the joy
I felt when I hid those envelopes
every week. This is paradise, but
that was the true meaning of joy."

In thinking about this story, I've often
wondered what was really involved in
Yosele's transformation from miser to holy
miser. How did he come to realize the need
to change not just his way of living, but his
way of experiencing life? For each of us, seeing where we are now is one of the most
challenging steps in getting where we want to
go. This self-assessment ought to be an
ongoing endeavor, even after we've made a

commitment toward becoming beings of sharing and have begun to make acts of sharing part of our daily lives. If you feel that you've reached the end of that process, the truth is you're probably still at the beginning. That's a good time to read this book again, as if you were reading it for the first time.

Similarly, there may be moments when the feeling of beginning anew may cause you to feel discouraged about your progress. You may sense that you have not yet gained the fulfillment you desire, and you may feel that it's because you're simply not performing enough sharing actions. But what's important is not just the number of things you do. It's your awareness of the direction in which you're going and of your desire to manifest the inner essence that brings oneness with the Creator.

In this continuing process of self-assessment and self-recognition, here are some questions that you may want to ask yourself.

Their purpose is not to criticize, but to help alert you to obstacles and areas you can work on as you become a being of sharing:

1. Do you expect others to give you a reward for sharing, even if you don't ask for one? This undercuts the power of your action to connect you with the Creator, who is never searching for a reward. Moreover, Kabbalah teaches that we acquire the limited happiness of physical rewards at the expense of true joy. This is precisely the reason that material gain never brings lasting satisfaction. We gain "things," but we forfeit the opportunity to fulfill our soul's yearning for connection to the Creator. So an act of sharing that contains a hidden agenda is not really a step toward the ultimate goal.

2. Have you made a "secret deal" with the Creator, whereby you'll perform acts of sharing in exchange for getting what you want in the material world? This, too, is something very different from living by The Secret.

3. Are you sharing so that others will like you?

4. Are you sharing because you think it's the moral thing to do, rather than because it fulfills your own deepest interest and your own true destiny?

5. Are you sharing because you're afraid you'll somehow be punished if you don't?

6. Are you only sharing when doing so is easy for you?

7. At every moment, even in tasks that seem utterly mundane and routine, are you aware of the opportunity to give and to share? Sharing means not just performing an action. It also means looking for the possibility of an action that will change an everyday situation into a manifestation of The Secret.

CHAPTER FOUR

LIVING THE SECRET

We've spoken about what The Secret is and what it requires, and we've seen some of the hidden complexities that transformative sharing can bring up. This chapter offers six specific steps to help you in your work of living The Secret. They are not listed in order of significance; one is as important as another. In fact, living The Secret means making *all* these points foundation principles in your life.

1. Bring a consciousness of sharing to everything you do. The Secret begins with altering the intention behind the things you're already doing. You don't have to try to communicate this to others or to reserve a consciousness of sharing for acts that seem "worthy" of it. Just know in your own heart that you intend to manifest The Secret.

2. As the intention to share becomes part of your moment-to-moment awareness, perform acts of sharing whenever, wherever, and however possible. The Secret is manifested through actions, and the rewards of those actions are expressed in every aspect of our lives—material, emotional, and spiritual—not just in the intellectual understanding of a principle.

3. With conscious awareness and attention, increase the intensity of sharing by searching for ways to make acts of sharing more and more challenging for yourself.

4. Keep a written record of your development toward becoming a being of sharing: your experiences, your thoughts, and your feelings. Of all the many things you can do to bring The Secret into your life, none is more powerful than recording your experiences and the responses they call up in your heart and your mind.

5. Read this book often to keep you constantly in touch with The Secret and remind you of the goal. Paradoxically, we're always at two places at once on our spiritual path.

We're always starting anew, no matter how far we may have come. The Secret is a starting point to which you should always be eager to return.

6. Not only is The Secret about sharing, but it is meant to be shared! So share The Secret with others in your life—not just by passing on this book, but by describing The Secret in your own words. Teaching is the best way to learn any subject, and sharing The Secret is a great chance to improve your own understanding of it.

Always remember that a life full of joy and fulfillment is your true destiny, and if your life is anything less, remember that the cause is always a loss of connection with the source of all joy. To reestablish that connection, you don't need to delve deep into your

past or repent your sins or become a vege-
tarian or get a high-paying job. All you need
are the six steps we've presented here.

CHAPTER FIVE

COMPLETING
THE PUZZLE

The Secret works because it unlocks the door to the joy and fulfillment ordained for us. This great truth was introduced in the first chapter of this book and we have alluded to it several times in various ways, but it needs to be repeated once again. By *learning* The Secret and by *living* it, you can achieve your life's true purpose. You should not settle for anything less.

We began with the story of Rav Ashlag's conversations with his spiritual master and the mysterious lesson that was passed from teacher to student. I described the compelling desire I felt to penetrate this mystery, find The Secret, and share that wisdom with the world. When I first set out on this path, I hoped I would have a sudden revelation. Perhaps I would find a long-lost letter or meet someone in whom Rav Ashlag had confided The Secret.

But the discovery was an unfolding rather than an epiphany. As I mentioned in Chapter 1, The Secret did not appear as a particular letter or document but as a process of enlightenment that included many elements. As a starting point, in carefully studying Rav Ashlag's writings, I saw how his development into the greatest Kabbalist of the 20th century really began when he learned The Secret from his anonymous master in Jerusalem. I've made a number of visits to Rav Ashlag's grave in Jerusalem, and I'm grateful for the deep insights these visits have brought me. I've also had the opportunity to use the tools and teachings of Kabbalah in the real world as a son, student, teacher, husband, father, brother, and friend. Most importantly, I've benefited from my parents, Rav Berg and Karen Berg, and from their living example of what sharing and oneness with the Creator really mean.

Some of my clearest childhood memories are of my parents' determination to spread the wisdom of Kabbalah. Many times they presented lectures to only two or three listeners. Today the Kabbalah Centre has fifty locations around the world, and every week tens of thousands of people study Kabbalah through the Centre's classes, events, or online at our website, Kabbalah.com. Literally millions of books on Kabbalah have been distributed around the world by the Kabbalah Centre, including translations into twenty languages. All this has taken place in just ten years. No one at the Kabbalah Centre takes credit for this. We know that the success of the Centre is an expression of the Creator's desire for our fulfillment. And now that The Secret, the essence of Kabbalistic teaching, is available to the world, we know also that the lives of even more people will be touched and enriched by the power of Kabbalah and The Secret.

Today I realize that my discovery of The Secret was like finding a golden key and much like completing a puzzle in which the last piece fell into place with a sense of rightness and inevitability. The Secret asks us to make a fundamental change in our consciousness—a transformation of our nature from *wanting and getting to giving and sharing*. As I have said, this is not easy. Yet the joy that The Secret brings is abundantly worth the effort—not only for ourselves as individuals but for all humanity.

By becoming beings of sharing, we share what we become with everyone. By completing the process of creation within ourselves, we can bring about its completion everywhere. We all have the task, therefore, not only of transforming ourselves as individuals but also of bringing about the world's transformation. By recognizing and achieving the true purpose of our lives, we can extinguish pain, suffering, and even death itself. The Creator intends and desires joy for us. Indeed, Kabbalah teaches that the Creator wants to bring us fulfillment even more than we want to receive it. I am certain in my heart that, with the help of The Secret, that divine wish will be fulfilled.

Now *you* are ready to start living The Secret. When you do this with an open heart and a sincere desire for joy and fulfillment, I know you will find millions of others joining you in this sacred endeavor, until The Secret and the joy that it brings is no longer a secret but the daily reality of all humanity.

TWO FINAL THOUGHTS

Here are two very useful principles to keep in mind as you put the lessons of this book into action. These are practical insights that have been of great help to me personally, and I continue to rely on them whenever the need arises. I believe you'll find these ideas of help as you bring The Secret into your life.

The degree of fulfillment you enjoy at any point in time depends on the strength of your connection to the Creator—and you yourself are responsible for that connection.

It's only natural to want more joy, more good health, more protection from negative influences, more prosperity, more opportunities to give and receive love. When you want more, the next step is simply to do more, always with the intent of creating connection with the Creator.

Whenever negativity appears in any area of your life, understand it as an indication that your connection with the Creator needs to be renewed and strengthened.

Remember: If your experience of life feels less than truly joyful, the fundamental cause is always a loss of connection with the source of all joy. Make a new commitment toward putting The Secret into action. You always have the power to eliminate negative energies completely from your life. When those energies are present, they tell you that you have lost your connection to the Creator, and they can therefore inspire you to rekindle that connection.

EPILOGUE

It is my hope that every person who reads this book will begin truly living The Secret and feel all the joy and fulfillment that it can bring.

It is my greater hope that, as The Secret becomes part of the world's consciousness, we can create a change in the world as a whole.

Imagine a world in which people know that sharing with others is the best way for them to achieve fulfillment. That taking for themselves will bring them only emptiness rather than joy. This is a world in which there will be no place for wars, strife, and pain.

As you begin seeing the fulfillment this book can bring you, I would ask you to think also of how the power of The Secret can benefit all humanity. Then take The Secret as I have tried to do and share it proactively with your friends and your family, or in any other way that spreads its joy and fulfillment.

If you would like to share with me any ideas on how to bring The Secret to the world, feel free to email me at thesecret@kabbalah.com.

May we all merit to live in a world where The Secret is known and lived by all, and where the joy and fulfillment we all deserve and are meant to receive is truly ours.

Blessings and Light,

Michael Berg

The latest from national best-selling author Michael Berg

Becoming Like God

At the age of 16, Kabbalistic scholar Michael Berg began the herculean task of translating the Zohar—Kabbalah's chief text—from its original Aramaic into its first complete English translation. The Zohar, which consists of 23 volumes, is considered a compendium of virtually all information pertaining to the universe, and its wisdom is only beginning to be verified today.

During the ten years he worked on the Zohar, Michael Berg discovered the long-lost secret for which mankind has searched for more than 5,000 years: how to acheive our ultimate destiny. *Becoming Like God* reveals the transformative method by which people can actually break free of what is called "ego nature" to achieve total joy and lasting life.

Berg puts forth the revolutionary idea that for the first time in history, an opportunity is being made available to humankind: an opportunity to Become Like God.

More products that can help you bring the wisdom of Kabbalah into your life

The 72 Names of God: Technology for the Soul™
—a national best-seller by author Yehuda Berg

The story of Moses and the Red Sea is well known to almost everyone; it's even been an Academy Award—winning film. What is not known, according to the internationally prominent Kabbalist Rabbi Yehuda Berg, is that a state-of-the-art technology is encoded and concealed within that biblical story. This technology is called the 72 Names of God, and it is the key—your key—to ridding yourself of depression, stress, creative stagnation, anger, illness, and other physical and emotional problems. In fact, the 72 Names of God is the oldest, most powerful tool known to mankind—far more powerful than any 21st century high-tech know-how when it comes to eliminating the garbage in your life so that you can wake up and enjoy life each day. Indeed, the 72 Names of God is the ultimate pill for anything and everything that ails you because it strikes at the DNA level of your soul.

The Power of Kabbalah
—an international best-seller by author Yehuda Berg

Imagine your life filled with unending joy, purpose, and contentment. Imagine your days infused with pure insight and energy. This is *The Power of Kabbalah*. It is the path from the momentary pleasure that most of us settle for to the lasting fulfillment that is yours to claim. Your deepest desires *are* waiting to be realized. But they are not limited to the temporary rush you might get from closing a business deal, the short-term high from drugs, or a passionate sexual relationship that lasts for only a few short months.

Wouldn't you like to experience a lasting sense of wholeness and peace that is unshakable, no matter what might be happening around you? Complete fulfillment is the promise of Kabbalah. Within these pages, you will learn how to look at and navigate through life in a whole new way. You will understand your purpose and how to receive the abundant gifts that are waiting for you. By making a critical transformation from a reactive to a proactive being, you will increase your creative energy, gain control of your life, and enjoy new spiritual levels of existence. Kabbalah's ancient teaching is rooted in the perfect union of the physical and spiritual laws already at work in your life. Get ready to experience this exciting realm of awareness, meaning, and joy.

The wonder and wisdom of Kabbalah have influenced the world's leading spiritual, philosophical, religious, and scientific minds. Until today, however, that wisdom was hidden away in ancient texts, available only to scholars who knew where to look. Now, after many centuries, *The Power of Kabbalah* resides in this one remarkable book. Here at long last is the complete and simple path—actions you can take right now to create the life you desire and deserve.

The Essential Zohar
By Rav Berg

The Zohar has traditionally been known as the world's most esoteric and profound spiritual document, but Rav Berg has dedicated his life to making this wisdom universally available. The vast wisdom and Light of the Zohar came into being as a gift to all humanity, and *The Essential Zohar* at last explains this gift to the world.

Audio Resources

The Power of Kabbalah Tape Series

The Power of Kabbalah is nothing less than a user's guide to the universe. Move beyond where you are right now to where you truly want to be—emotionally, spiritually, and creatively. This exciting tape series brings you the ancient, authentic teaching of Kabbalah in a powerful, practical audio format.

Creating Miracles in Your Life

We're used to thinking of a miracle as something that happens at the whim of God. But the Kabbalists have long taught that the true power to create miracles is present in each and every one of us—if only we can learn to access that power and put it into practice. This inspiring tape series shows how to do exactly that. Order it now, and enter the zone of the miraculous!

THE ZOHAR

"Bringing the Zohar from near oblivion to wide accessibility has taken many decades. It is an achievement of which we are truly proud and grateful."
—Michael Berg

Composed more than 2,000 years ago, the Zohar is a set of 23 books, a commentary on biblical and spiritual matters in the form of conversations among spiritual masters. But to describe the Zohar only in physical terms is greatly misleading. In truth, the Zohar is nothing less than a powerful tool for achieving the most important purposes of our lives. It was given to all humankind by the Creator to bring us protection, to connect us with the Creator's Light, and ultimately to fulfill our birthright of true spiritual transformation.

Eighty years ago, when the Kabbalah Centre was founded, the Zohar had virtually disappeared from the world. Few people in the general population had ever heard of it. Whoever sought to read it—in any country, in any language, at any price—faced a long and futile search.

Today all this has changed. Through the work of the Kabbalah Centre and the editorial efforts of Michael Berg, the Zohar is now being brought to the world, not only in the original Aramaic language but also in English.

The new English Zohar provides everything for connecting to this sacred text on all levels: the original Aramaic text for scanning; an English translation; and clear, concise commentary for study and learning.

THE KABBALAH CENTRE
The International Leader
in the Education of Kabbalah

Since its founding, the Kabbalah Centre has had a single mission: to improve and transform people's lives by bringing the power and wisdom of Kabbalah to all who wish to partake of it.

Through the lifelong efforts of Rav Berg, his wife Karen, and the great spiritual lineage of which they are a part, an astonishing 3.5 million people around the world have already been touched by the powerful teachings of Kabbalah. And each year, the numbers are growing!

As the leading source of Kabbalistic wisdom with 50 locations around the world, the Kabbalah Centre offers you a wealth of resources, including:

- The English Zohar, the first-ever comprehensive English translation of the foundation of Kabbalistic wisdom. In 23 beautifully bound volumes, this edition includes the full Aramaic text, the English translation, and detailed commentary, making this once-inaccessible text understandable to all.

- A full schedule of workshops, lectures, and evening classes for students at all levels of knowledge and experience.

- CDs, audiotapes and videotapes, and books in English and ten other languages.

- One of the Internet's most exciting and comprehensive websites, **www.kabbalah.com**—which receives more than 100,000 visitors each month.

- A constantly expanding list of events and publications to help you live *The Secret* and other teachings of Kabbalah with greater understanding and excitement.

Discover why the Kabbalah Centre is one of the world's fastest-growing spiritual organizations. Our sole purpose is to improve people's lives through the teachings of Kabbalah. Let us show you what Kabbalah can do for you!

Each Kabbalah Centre location hosts free introductory lectures. For more information on Kabbalah or on these and other products and services, call 1-800-KABBALAH.

Wherever you are, there's a Kabbalah Centre—because now you can call 1-800-KABBALAH from almost anywhere, 18 hours a day, and get answers or guidance right over the telephone. You'll be connected to distinguished senior faculty who are on hand to help you understand Kabbalah as deeply as you want to—whether it involves recommending a course of study; deciding which books/tapes to take or the order in which to take them; discussing the material; or anything else you wish to know about Kabbalah.